While Christians Sleep…

Willis A. Bullard

ISBN-13: 978-1492133131

ISBN-10: 1492133132

DEDICATION

NOT TO US OH LORD, BUT TO THY
NAME GIVE GLORY!

KNOWLEDGE CHECK i

Prologue...3

Identifying evil 8

The First Commandment 25

The Second Commandment 32

The Third Commandment...39

The fourth commandment 45

The Fifth Commandment 53

The Sixth Commandment 59

The Seventh Commandment 68

The Eighth Commandment 74

The Ninth Commandment 81

The Tenth Commandment...87

Can we live under the Ten Commandments?..............94

Matthew 22:36-39 97

KNOWLEDGE CHECK

Place a word or phrase that summarizes each of these Commandments:

1st Commandment

2nd Commandment

3rd Commandment

4th Commandment

5th Commandment

6th Commandment

7th Commandment

8th Commandment

9th Commandment

10th Commandment

PROLOGUE

It is clear by watching the news on television or reading the headlines of the printed news, our world is in or nearing a state of chaos and disorder. But what is more troubling is how we are addressing the chaos or more accurately how we are not addressing the chaos. How we, as a society, insist on watering down the problems or finding different justifications for the turmoil we experience daily instead of addressing the issues head on. The main issue is we are slowly becoming a sin-dominated society and Christians are largely to blame.

Well this is not the happiest of opening paragraphs, but then again, this is a book that is not meant to pat us on the back. This is a call to action; a plea for Christians to wake up and start acting out the words they are professing. And please do not say "who is he to judge?" because I am not judging, I will be pointing out facts and pointing fingers at myself the entire way. Matter of fact, I have been working on this book for a long time and the reality is I have had to stop writing and spend countless hours, days and even weeks praying and asking God to heal my hurt and redirect my life.

So the question at hand is this: Can a person live in today's society observing the laws as detailed in the Ten Commandments? I mean it sounds like a no brainer given the Christian nature of our country, but just how hard can living "under the law" be in this society?

Now in my eyes, the main problem with our world today is the bitter reality that evil is trying to take over our country by muting Christians and other God fearing people. That is why I took on this mission to see if it is possible to live as a Christian in today's world and follow the Ten Commandments. I also wanted to find out are the Commandments still relevant and are Christians the minority.

My research has been an incredible journey in which I have learned so much about God, myself, and a sobering fact that Christianity is still alive but almost on life-support.

Trinity College, in the beautiful state of Connecticut conducted a study that revealed the majority of people living in the United States (76% to 80%) identify themselves as Protestants or Catholics, accounting for 51% and 25% of the population respectively.

Another poll, this one by Mark Chaves, a Duke University professor of religion and divinity, found that 92% of Americans believed in God.

Really? If these studies are true, and I have no

doubt they are, then much of the "get God out of society" movement is being driven by 8% of Americans who do not believe in God or a god. And for those confused by what you just read, I am referring to the movement that removed prayer from school. The movements that want to eliminate public displays of the Ten Commandments. The misguided movements to remove the cross from cemeteries and memorials. The renaming of Christmas trees to Holiday trees. Schools insisting their students will be taking winter break instead of a Christmas break. Local officials not allowing the Menorah or Nativity from being displayed on government property.

I see the removal of God from our society as the work of the evil one, satan. I originally wanted to title this book "The Devil Works Overtime" but I didn't want to give the author of evil a headline of any type. Evil already dominates our headlines and more and more we have become numb to the true identity of evil.

Most days or nights I listen to the headlines of the day on the television before sitting down to study as I complete this devotional. It is these headlines that have prompted me to say enough is enough. All these experts on the news dissecting the atrocities of the shootings in Colorado and Connecticut. Blaming everything from video games to parenting, or even blaming society for ignoring people who are different. Such garbage! What we have here, ladies and gentlemen, is a sin problem. Nothing more, nothing less. Our society has turned a blind eye to sin. Mostly under the guise of political correctness or human rights. It was the Christian music group **dc Talk** that said it best in their song 'Socially Acceptable' - *"Times are changing, with morals in decay, human rights have made the wrongs okay. Something's missing, and if you're asking me, I think that something is the G-O-D."*

So whatever your political affiliation, your denomination, your religious view, or your spiritual view, this book should be read with an open mind. It is not my intent to convert anyone, that is the job of the Holy Spirit. It is not my intent to talk poorly about denominations, God handles that shameful area of Christianity. No, it is my intent to point out the obvious – we are drowning in sin and in order to stay above water we need to embrace the Laws of God. It is my prayer that we get everyone to start looking at today's world through the eyes of truth. I want you, the reader, to realize there is only good or evil; right or wrong. We have strayed so far from that single truth that Christianity has almost become irrelevant.

The Bible has been transformed from being God's Living Word to just another book that many use as a coffee table display in their homes. The Ten Commandments have become suggestions and sin is now a lucrative business and a normal way of life. It is almost as if evil has challenged our society to see how many of the Ten Commandments we can break while on earth.

Disagree with me if you must. I do not declare this

book to be Gospel or the end all answers to all our problems. I just want to wake up the Christian population that is slowly becoming satisfied with their pious existence consisting of going to church for four hours on a Sunday and acknowledging their love for God with their "country club" friends, and then turning around and living in drastic contradiction with what they professed.

Because while Christians sleep, all around the world, evil continues to do its work to destroy God's creation and derail His perfect plan. We have been lured into a slumber by daily rituals. Pushed into a spiritual coma with which we are now becoming accustomed. We just sit back and wait for Sunday.

Again the key question: Can people live in this society in obedience to the Ten Commandments? Well the first step is to consider how important the Ten Commandments are to our daily lives. The Ten Commandments teach us about life in God's kingdom, guiding us on our journey. The purpose of the law is not to show us what we must do to receive God's grace, rather they show us how we should live as a people who know the grace of God. These are not unattainable goals or impossible codes of conduct to live by; they are, however, the first steps towards discipleship on the glorious, God-led path to eternal life.

IDENTIFYING EVIL

When I reviewed the different surveys and polls regarding Christianity, belief in God or gods, church attendance, etcetera, I found it a bit amusing to see that on many of the polls there was a category labeled "unsure" or "don't know". I stared at a 2006 CBS News Poll of adults in the United States with results that found 76% of those surveyed believed in a god, while 9% believed in "some other universal spirit" or "higher power", 8% believed in neither, and 1% were unsure.

Please understand, I am not a genius. I joke with teens and young adults I work with that my score of 32 on the ACT was a cumulative score of the three times I took the test. But I am an accomplished researcher and analyst. During my research I was flabbergasted at the fact that there are those who can claim to be unsure of whether or not they believe in a god or spiritual higher power. And then I experienced the ultimate mind-twist when, during this research, I also found such entities as the Church of the Jedi, and a Sponge Bob Worship Center. WOW! And I thought after being a youth pastor I had seen everything.

So with the uncertainty of some people in the

existence of God, I was sure that everyone would still accept that there was good and bad. That shouldn't be hard to determine would it?

The definition of evil, you would think, would be a cut and dry almost elementary definition to share. Not so. Most dictionaries list evil as: 1. morally wrong or bad; immoral; wicked: *evil deeds; an evil life.* 2. harmful; injurious: *evil laws.* 3. characterized or accompanied by misfortune or suffering; unfortunate; disastrous: *to be fallen on evil days.* 4. due to actual or imputed bad conduct or character: *an evil reputation.* 5. marked by anger, irritability, irascibility, etc.: *He is known for his evil disposition.*

But then there are other sites that want to chime in on their version of evil. I found many churches and denominations had their specific definition of evil. And then there are the completely unbelievable sites listing all-time top-ten evil and good people. I apparently did not make either list, which is a good thing (at least not being on the evil list).

But all these different views of evil is troubling to me because growing up on the Gulf Coast of Florida I remember being taught evil is the opposite of good. It was cut and dry and easy to discern. But therein lies the problem with today's world. We want to understand evil as being 'not good' but our society has blurred the definition of good so much that evil is now almost unknown or at least unrecognizable as evil.

Maybe it is just me and other Christians who are

overreacting and reading too much into this 'evil running rampant' thing, because that is what my Atheist acquaintances tell me. But then I find glimmers of hope. One such moment was when I read the words of one of America's greatest news anchors, Mr. Ted Koppel, during a commencement speech at Duke University – "*Our society finds truth too strong a medicine to digest undiluted. In its purest form, truth is not a polite tap on the shoulder; it is a howling reproach. What Moses brought down from Mount Sinai were not the Ten Suggestions; they are Commandments. Are, not were. The sheer beauty of the Commandments is that they codify in a handful of words acceptable human behavior, not just for then or now, but for all time.*"[i]

Cut and dry. But we did not see that air on the news. An icon of the news industry acknowledging the importance of the Ten Commandments. Alas, I continued my research and stumbled upon what I believe to be the best definition of evil:

> Evil is commonly associated with conscious and deliberate wrongdoing, or deliberately disobeying the commandments of a god or gods, or the rules of society; discrimination designed to harm others; humiliation of people designed to diminish their psychological well-being and dignity; destructiveness; motives of causing pain or suffering for selfish or malicious intentions; and acts of unnecessary or indiscriminate violence[ii].

By accepting this definition, it is clear that there is

an unmistakable difference between evil and good. To further our understanding, let us take each part of this definition and explore it a little further.

First, "conscious and deliberate wrongdoing, disobeying the commandments of a god or gods, or the rules of society." What this breaks down to is a willful or purposed behavior to do what is wrong. Taking an "I want to do wrong" attitude. And although some would argue that deciding what is wrong is a herculean task, I like how it is written in the definition. The first part tells us disobeying the commandments of a god or gods is wrong. But who are these gods? Let's explore these traditions. Most religions and denominations which defines commandments of a god or gods are much like the traditional Christian belief in the Ten Commandments. These commandments are the Ten Laws that are listed in the Old Testament of the Holy Bible or within the writings of the Hebrew Bible, specifically the Torah. But over the years, these commandments have either been watered down or changed altogether making them, in essence the Ten Suggestions.

The Ten Commandments have been a point of contention between religious sects for centuries. These words of law first appear in the book of Exodus and later in the book of Deuteronomy and as you will read, controversy began at the introduction of these laws.

The common story of the revelation of these laws

begins in Exodus 19 after the arrival of the people of Israel at Mount Sinai. Remember, these are the people that Moses was ordained to lead out of Egypt. To summarize the story we see:

In the morning of the "third day" of their encampment, "*there was thunder and lightning, and a thick cloud upon the mountain, and the voice of the trumpet exceedingly loud*", and the people assembled at the base of the mount. After "*the LORD came down upon Mount Sinai,*" Moses went up briefly and returned and prepared the people.

And then in Exodus 20 "***God spoke***" to all the people the words of the covenant.

Did you catch that? ***God spoke*** the Ten Commandments to the people of Israel as they were traveling through the wilderness. And even though the people heard the voice of God, they became afraid to hear more and moved away. Even Moses said, "*I exceedingly fear and quake.*" Thankfully, Moses drew near the thick darkness to hear the additional laws, (Exodus 21–23) all which he wrote in the book of the covenant which he read to the people the next morning, and they agreed to be obedient and do all the LORD had said.

Moses then escorted a select group consisting of "*seventy of the elders of Israel*" to a location on the mount where they worshipped and they "*saw the God of Israel above a paved work like clear sapphire stone.*" (Exodus 24:1-11)

The mount was covered by the cloud for six days,

after which Moses went into the midst of the cloud and was "*in the mount forty days and forty nights.*" (Exodus 24:16-18)

Before the full forty days expired, the people of Israel decided that something happened to Moses, and compelled Aaron to fashion a golden calf, and he "*built an altar before it*" (Exodus32:1–5), and the people worshipped the calf. (Exodus 32:6–8) After the full forty days, Moses and Joshua came down from the mountain with the tablets of stone: "*And it came to pass, as soon as he came nigh unto the camp, that he saw the calf, and the dancing, and Moses' anger waxed hot, and he cast the tablets out of his hands, and broke them beneath the mount.*" (Exodus 32:19) After the events in chapters 32 and 33, the LORD told Moses, to form two tablets of stone like the first, and "*I will write upon these tables the words that were in the first tablets, which thou hast broken.*" (Exodus 34:1)

According to Jewish tradition, Exodus 20:1–17 is God's first speaking and writing down of the ten commandments on the two tablets, which were broken in pieces by Moses. These Commandments were later rewritten on replacement stones and placed in the ark of the covenant. Deuteronomy 5:4–20 details God's re-telling of the ten commandments to the younger generation who were to enter the promised land.

But as you see, evil presented itself immediately upon hearing the law. Fear and doubt overcame those who actually **heard** the voice of God. So what did they do? The sent Moses to be the spokesperson because, just like us, sometimes we do not want to hear the truth. Once their leader was absent, they decided to deliberately disobey the first of the laws they had heard. Isn't this a picture of what we are today? Where were the voices of those who did not want to follow the bad crowd? Why did they sit quietly and allow the evil and debauchery to take place?

Well God's plan was not thwarted. And Moses said, "the LORD delivered unto me two tablets of stone written with the finger of God; and on them was written according to all the words, which the LORD spoke with you in the mount out of the midst of the fire in the day of the assembly." (Deuteronomy 9:10)

"And he wrote on the tablets, according to the first writing, the ten commandments, which the LORD spoke unto you in the mount out of the midst of the fire in the day of the assembly: and the LORD gave them unto me." (Deuteronomy 10:4)

Here are the Ten Commandments as documented for us in Deuteronomy Chapter 5:6-21

[6] *"I am the Lord your God, who brought you out of Egypt, out of the land of slavery.*
[7] *"You shall have no other gods before me.*
[8] *"You shall not make for yourself an image in the form of anything in heaven above or on the earth beneath or in the waters below. [9] You shall not bow down to them or worship*

them; for I, the Lord your God, am a jealous God, punishing the children for the sin of the parents to the third and fourth generation of those who hate me, [10] but showing love to a thousand generations of those who love me and keep my commandments.

[11] "You shall not misuse the name of the Lord your God, for the Lord will not hold anyone guiltless who misuses his name.

[12] "Observe the Sabbath day by keeping it holy, as the Lord your God has commanded you. [13] Six days you shall labor and do all your work, [14] but the seventh day is a Sabbath to the Lord your God. On it you shall not do any work, neither you, nor your son or daughter, nor your male or female servant, nor your ox, your donkey or any of your animals, nor any foreigner residing in your towns, so that your male and female servants may rest, as you do. [15] Remember that you were slaves in Egypt and that the Lord your God brought you out of there with a mighty hand and an outstretched arm. Therefore the Lord your God has commanded you to observe the Sabbath day.

[16] "Honor your father and your mother, as the Lord your God has commanded you, so that you may live long and that it may go well with you in the land the Lord your God is giving you.

[17] "You shall not murder.

[18] "You shall not commit adultery.

[19] "You shall not steal.

[20] "You shall not give false testimony against your neighbor.

[21] "You shall not covet your neighbor's wife. You shall not set your desire on your neighbor's house or land, his male or female servant, his ox or donkey, or anything that belongs to your neighbor."

Keeping in mind my pathetic poor performance on the ACT score and the fact that I am not a seventy-pound head genius sitting in a research facility studying these words at length... I must confess to you – I get this! I can really understand the Ten Commandments as they are presented here in Scripture, well at least the Ten Commandments I came to understand over the years of my life. But I also realize that growing up hearing the Ten Commandments and watching it on the television every Easter on the epic movie with Charlton Heston and by reading it every now and then, it is easy to see why the Ten Commandments have been interpreted and misinterpreted in so many different ways.

Some of the Commandments are straight forward with little to no room for misinterpretation. You know the easy ones like do not kill or do not commit adultery, or even do not steal. But take a closer look at these words and discover that even with these cut and dry commandments, there are churches that have decided to redefine the words to fit their own ideology. And because of this, our understanding has been somewhat skewed. Scholars also caution us that through the multiple translations and cultural changes, some of these commandments are not as crystal clear as we think.

Different Bible translations set aside; one thing we can be sure about is that evil is the conscious and deliberate disobedience to these laws and any actions leading to the deliberate or conscious disobedience constitutes an evil action.

God entered into a contract with the children of Israel when He presented them with the Ten Commandments. When you enter into a contract, both sides must fulfill their part of the agreement so that the contract is completed. But man has never fulfilled his part of the agreement. The children of Israel fell short and because of that, a penalty had to be paid. Enter Jesus.

Jesus came and lived a perfect life under the Covenant or Contract of Moses and thereby fulfilled man's part of the covenant. Just as man was condemned because of the sinful life of one man, man was also restored by the sinless life of one man, fulfilling the covenant and paying the penalty for the indiscretions of Adam and all men on the cross.

By living a perfect life under the law, Jesus was justified under the law. By sacrificing Himself on the cross Jesus paid the penalty that we should have paid. Our journey is to discover whether we can live today, under laws given to us long ago. Times have changed and we need to identify how the players have changed. God has remained the same: *"I am the Alpha and the Omega," says the Lord God, "who is and who was and who is to come, the Almighty."* Revelation 1:8

It is evil that changes. We can define and identify evil by understanding the laws followed by those who believe in God. And this includes, but certainly is not limited to Judaism, Christianity, Roman Catholicism, and Lutheranism. But how about believers who do not take the Ten Commandments as their law? What laws or commandments do the other 'god's' say?

Now keeping in mind that we are looking at evil as commonly associated with conscious and deliberate wrongdoing and disobeying the commandments of a god or gods, let's take a look at other beliefs.

The Buddhist ethics dictate that evil means "whatever harms or obstructs the causes for happiness in this life". Instead of evil and good, the Buddhist uses the words suffering and enlightenment which I think is a slightly stronger way to describe these acts. However, within the Buddhist belief system there are catalogued causes to suffering. The Buddha acknowledged that there is both happiness and sorrow in the world, but he taught that even when we have some kind of happiness, it is not permanent; it is subject to change. And due to this unstable, impermanent nature of all things, everything we experience is said to have the quality of **duhkha** or an unsatisfactory state of being. Therefore unless we can gain insight into that truth, and understand what is really able to provide lasting happiness, and what is unable to provide happiness, the experience of dissatisfaction will persist. In essence, whatever causes you this state of suffering, other than ordinary suffering, known as **duhkha-duhkha** (the physical suffering or pain associated with giving birth, growing old, physical illness and the process of dying), all those other causes of suffering can be considered evil[iii].

In Hinduism the concept of Dharma or truth or righteousness clearly divides the world into good and evil, and clearly explains that wars have to be waged sometimes to establish and protect Dharma (truth). This division of good and evil is of major importance in both the Hindu epics of Ramayana and Mahabharata. In whatever way a Hindu defines the goal of life or truth, there are several methods (called yogas) that the Hindu teacher or sage teaches for reaching that goal. Each way brings the believer to an inner soul search so that anything that moves against this harmonious existence or zero-karma, is evil and not needed. It is more a path to devotion and selfless action than an act of faith[iv].

Within Islam, it is considered essential to believe that all comes from Allah, whether it is perceived as good or bad by individuals; and those things that are perceived as evil or bad are either natural events or caused by a person's free will to disobey the orders of Allah. Muslims believe evil is anything that is contrary to given laws. All Muslim scholars agree upon seven major sins which are considered **kaba'ir**. These sins are called the Pernicious Seven or the Deadly Seven (sins). However, there are an additional seventy major sins that are a collection of deeds of varying degrees of offensiveness that have been compiled by religious muslim scholars after Mohammed's time, according to the beliefs of their respective periods. But again, these are listed and any participation in any of the listed sins is considered evil[v]. I mention this list has grown or has been added onto over the years since the death of Mohammed only because it is my belief that this is the genesis of the radicalization of the Islamic faith.

So we see the major religions of the world, those believing in God or a god, have a clear definition of what is considered evil and for the most part, they too closely parallel the Ten Commandments, if not verbatim, clearly through the intent of the laws.

Once again, the definition of evil from the popular world wide web site, Wikipedia is: Evil is commonly associated with conscious and deliberate wrongdoing, disobeying the commandments of a god or gods, or the rules of society, discrimination designed to harm others, humiliation of people designed to diminish their psychological well-being and dignity, destructiveness, motives of causing pain or suffering for selfish or malicious intentions, and acts of unnecessary or indiscriminate violence

Clearly, when we read 'discrimination designed to harm others, humiliation of people designed to diminish their psychological well-being and dignity, destructiveness, motives of causing pain or suffering for selfish or malicious intentions' this covers just about everything we see or experience in our society today. From racism to bullying it is clear evil is a deliberate action that causes others pain or suffering. But one has to wonder; if this is a valid definition of what evil is, then sadly evil is spread farther and greater than we can imagine.

Evil has become the new norm in our society. Look around and see the influences of evil versus the influences of good. We can see the overt display of evil when we see the unconscionable acts of violence like we have seen in the Connecticut School shootings or the Colorado movie theater shooting or the Virginia Tech shooting. It is easy to see the manifestation of evil in the countless child abuse cases or kidnappings.

But it is the covert side of evil that is destroying our society. Covert actions that have lead to our lethargic attitude which allows bad things to continue to happen. We have sat back and allowed questionable material to be transmitted over all forms of mass media from television airways to the world wide web. How? Because the author of evil, the devil, is slick and knows how to gently pick away at the fabric of all that is innocent until it is spoiled by evil.

Where is this evil? Sadly it is everywhere and spreading. The slap in the face is evil has been picking away at the fabric of decency in such a soft and surreptitious way that many have not even noticed the change.

We live in a fast-paced, never sleeping, world. It never stops to observe a Sabbath. Our idols are very real, if less obvious than they were in the days of Moses. As a society, we worship money, sex, and power and, with the help of 'Reality Television', we celebrate these "little 'g' gods" daily. Most of us have a much different understanding of religious tolerance, marriage and divorce, parent and child relationships, physical and psychological motives. But society exploits all these for the sake of entertainment.

Coveting is considered a good thing because it drives our economy. We all want to keep up with the Joneses or even become the Joneses. Our desires are controlled by advertisers that tell us how incomplete our lives are without their products. Adultery sells lots of magazines, DVD's, and television time. The most popular trend is to blame all problems on parents or other societal groups. Lying and stealing is commonplace in business and politics and we might as well admit that lying has become acceptable unless (or until) you get caught. We have removed God from the public arena, except as an exclamation of surprise, as in OMG. The lives of the people making the most noise over how they are offended by the posting the Ten Commandments in public places are often the best witness as to why the Ten Commandments are ignored. If we are really honest with ourselves, it is hard to find evidence that anyone takes the Ten Commandments seriously at all. So what is a faithful Christian to do? How do we incorporate God's Commandments into our lives and still live in this world? Does God have authority in the modern world?

And now our journey begins. Let us explore the Ten Commandments and reflect on how these commandments fit in our lives. I encourage you to study this alone during your quiet time or share with a

Bible study group. You will be tempted to read it in one sitting, but I implore you to take your time and reflect on each of the chapters. Take time to consider your role in God's plan. And whenever possible, please seek out a Bible loving church or a Bible loving spiritual leader should you have any questions. Our society is slowly coming unraveled and although we know how the story ends, God's Master Plan does include and require the participation of us, His children.

Willis A. Bullard

THE FIRST COMMANDMENT

Recommended Scripture Readings: Psalm 117; Jeremiah 10; John 4

THOU SHALT HAVE NO OTHER GODS BEFORE ME (KJV).

There are 613 commandments in the Old Testament. And in terms of chronological order "Thou shalt have no other gods before me" is certainly not the first commandment. Chronologically, the first actual commandment in the Old Testament is found in Genesis 1:28 "*Be fruitful and multiply*".

However, the Hebrew word that we translate "first" (as in first Commandment) means not just numerically first but first in importance. This pushes the chronologically first commandment of being fruitful and multiplying to number 125 - and now you have a great trivia fact. But the fact still remains, we have an order of commandments and they are based on their importance. As we apply this to the Ten

Commandments, Jesus clarified his stance by saying to love God with all your heart is not only the first but also the "greatest" Commandment. Did you all catch that?

The number one rule, according to Jesus Christ, is to place no other god before The Creator of the Universe – God the Father. Now for the atheist this is a non-problem, or so they think. But for the majority of the American population, and the World population for that matter, this means that God is God and there can be no other placed before him. He is the Supreme Being, the Major Deity and He Is the creator who IS.

But if you just read the Ten Commandments as part of your Bible study time, you neglect to dive in and discover the strength in other verses throughout the Bible but, in relation to the Ten Commandments, verses in Exodus Chapter 20 before the Commandments begin: *And God spoke all these words: "I am the Lord your God, who brought you out of Egypt, out of the land of slavery.*

To those of the Jewish faith, this is their first Commandment. To this day many of the Jewish sages teach the greatest of all the *mitzvoth* (Commandments) is the Commandment, "I am the LORD your God". Why is that first to them? Because we need to understand some of the words that were translated. *God spoke all these words* – 'words' is a loose interpretation of instructions. They were not just words, they were Commandments and the first words he spoke were: *I am the Lord your God.* The Jewish faith believe that until we are really willing to accept Adonai[vi] as our God, as he has commanded, the rest of the Commandments are not likely to be obeyed because, quite frankly, without that core belief in Gods' sovereignty, the Commandments are worthless. The God of Israel is calling us to obey the glorious truth that He is our God.

Too often we have doubted the existence of God with such arguments as: if God exists and has dominion over us, why does he allow all this suffering, doesn't He care? God does care. He knows when we suffer; and although many will try to explain this by comparing it with the love of your dad and how he never let bad things happen to you, we have to remember God isn't a mere human. He is God. His perspective is infinitely greater than ours. He sees the "bigger picture" that our puny mortal human minds will never understand. However painful or unhappy our experiences, His will is to lead us on a path to our eventual benefit.

Having experienced loss and tragedy in my life, I understand that there are times when Christians will question God's existence. Through every significant emotional and physical event I have gone through, I look back and realize how God was there to help me through what I believed was an unfixable problem, and in one case, an almost life ending tragedy. Our mortal minds cannot fathom what is yet to come.

But society hands us so many replacements for

God in our lives. Our jobs, our toys (cars, boats, etc.), even our families can all work their way into our lives as more important than God. These things can become our God if we allow them to become too great in our lives. And as innocent as adoring these things may seem, it is the evil ones way of taking God away from His proper place of being the most important aspect of our life.

But take a look at where we are today as a society. Church pews empty on Sunday's. Christian book stores struggling to stay open while I have yet to see a liquor store going out of business. Political leaders and organizations trying to impose their will upon our religious beliefs. What are we going to do when we are told to bow down before our country's leader instead of God? We already lift up Hollywood actors to the level of deity.

Our first Commandment is to have no other God before our Creator. I remember the days when God was honored and respected in our society. In the late 1960's and through the 1970's my school day started with the Pledge of Allegiance and a moment of prayer. Can we return to those days? I believe so, but we have become lazy as Christians and sometimes we cannot follow a Commandment as easy as this one.

So I wondered, why did God have to speak these laws to his people or better yet, why did he have to write the laws down for mankind? Scripture shows us that God was seeing that man's track record was not that great. First Adam and Eve succumbed to the temptations of the evil one; years pass and every thought of man became evil and God flooded the planet save one righteous man, Noah and his family; and now his people that He freed from Egypt were going astray. But God loves them so much, He reminds them of the Laws already written in their hearts. God's Laws for man are spiritual laws and we, as spiritual beings, have the laws written on our hearts just as they were on the hearts of all the Israelites. And like the Israelites, God may have to remind us of these Laws because sin has once again blemished the heart of man.

The Israelites received this reminder from God which was actually a command to return to the love needed to be with God. Kind of like a do-over. But without a genuine love for God in our heart, obedience of the law is hypocrisy. The Israelites knew they were living in sin, that is why they were afraid when they heard the voice of God and they ran.

But God gives us the power to decide freely which path we follow. He gifted us the ability to think and perceive intuitively – we know right from wrong. And in return for this gift, if we focus our efforts on the One True God and place no others ahead of Him, we then are ultimately free.

Can we live in this world and follow God's Laws; Yes we can with this warning: following God is not for the weak. It requires action on our part. Let us become champions for God by placing no "thing" above Him.

Reflection:

1. What are your thoughts on the Jewish Faith taking *"And God spoke all these words: "I am the Lord your God, who brought you out of Egypt, out of the land of slavery." As their first Commandment?*

2. In your life, have you ever put something ahead of your love for God?

3. If you have not already done so, are you willing to make the commitment to live under the Law in the First Commandment?

THE SECOND COMMANDMENT

Recommended Scripture Readings: Exodus 34; Habakkuk 2; John 14:6-11

THOU SHALT NOT MAKE UNTO THEE ANY GRAVEN IMAGE (KJV).

This is one of the Commandments that has been a point of contention between denominations: *"You shall not make for yourself an idol in the form of anything in heaven above or on the earth beneath or in the waters below. You shall not bow down to them or worship them; for I, the Lord your God, am a jealous God, punishing the children for the sin of the fathers to the third and fourth generation of those who hate me, but showing love to a thousand generations of those who love me and keep my commandments."* Deuteronomy 5:8-10 NIV.

In the first commandment we are told *"Thou shalt have no other gods before Me."* Why does God command us not to have other gods before Him? Well because He is a jealous God *"for you shall not worship any other god, for the* LORD, *whose name is Jealous, is a jealous God"* Exodus 34:14, which suggests that He watches us lovingly and closely, like a faithful and passionate groom watches over his bride to be. Not like the stalker some may want to portray him as. He loves us and has given Himself to us fully and passionately; He is entirely committed to our relationship with Him.

Now here in the second Commandment we are forbidden to make any image of God *"With whom, then, will you compare God? To what image will you liken him?"* Isaiah 40:18.

We are also forbidden to make the image of any creature for a religious use. It is called the changing of the truth of God into a lie *"They exchanged the truth about God for a lie, and worshiped and served created things rather than the Creator who is forever praised."* Romans 1:25. This practice of making these graven images insinuates that God has a body, whereas the Holy Scripture tells us he is an infinite spirit, *"Of what value is an idol carved by a craftsman? Or an image that teaches lies? For the one who makes it trusts in his own creation; he makes idols that cannot speak".* Habakkuk 2:18. It also forbids us to make images of God in our own image, as if he were a man.

In short, you cannot "create" an image of God for the purpose of worshipping that image. When God created man in His image, it was the spiritual image of God that we were given not a physical likeness. This image gives us the ability to live a life fully and wholly pleasing to Him with a spirit that rejects sin.

Unfortunately, that spirit was busted when Adam and Eve decided to fall for the deceitfulness of evil and take away the innocence of the pure spirit.

The sin we inherited from Adam is the same sin the children of Israel took with them into the desert. God took his chosen people and entered into a Covenant that should they follow His Commands, they would surely enter the promised land. That deal was broken and mankind had to pay for their foolishness. But instead of you and I or any of the children of Israel paying for breaking the contract, God, in His infinite wisdom and with Love unmatched, sent Jesus to pay that price.

Jesus' role on Earth was also an example for us to follow. You see, had Jesus come to Earth in the manner in which he deserved, there would have been no manger. Instead, as a King, his life would have been one of great privilege, riches, and no suffering. But instead, God sent His son into the world just as He sent you and I. So that we may see, by this great example, that a sinless man can exist on this planet. No, we can never be sinless, but we can live a life free of deliberate sin.

For now we have a renewed contract that starts off with: "*For God so loved the world that he gave his one and only Son, that whoever believes in him shall not perish but have eternal life.*" John 3:16

It is not a graven image we need in our lives to secure our rightful place in eternity. We need only to focus on a spiritual existence with God. And with our spiritual relationship with God, we do not need to pray to any substitute or false God. He provides for our every need. We have the privilege of communicating directly with the Father because His love for us is so great He never leaves our side.

So is it wrong to hang a crucifix on your rear view mirror or place a picture of Jesus on the mantle over the fireplace? Absolutely not! This is not about using art or placards as a form of adoration. This is about replacing God with material items and turning our faith and trust into false gods.

I have a picture of Jesus in my house along with a collection of crucifixes hanging on the wall. Do I pray to them or do I believe they have magical powers? No. But they are beautiful both artistically and emotionally as each cross has a story on when they were presented to me.

But let me slow down and take a breath. Sometimes as we examine scripture we get engrossed by our own passions and desires and forget that God's living Word will speak to the open heart.

"You shall not make for yourself an idol, whether in the form of anything that is in heaven above, or that is on the earth beneath, or that is in the water under the earth. You shall not bow down to them or worship them; for I the LORD your God am a jealous God, punishing children for the iniquity of parents, to the third and the fourth generation of those who reject me, but showing steadfast love to the thousandth generation of those who love me and keep my commandments" Exodus 20:4-6.

If we go with a straight-up Old Testament view of the second commandment it is clear that God cannot and may not be visibly portrayed in any way.

But according to Scripture, Jesus Christ is *"the reflection of God's glory and the exact imprint of God's very being"* (Hebrews 1:3); he is *"the image of the invisible God"* (Colossians 1:15); so that *"whoever has seen Jesus has seen the Father"* (John 14:9).

So God can be portrayed visibly and God has been portrayed visibly. Jesus Christ is the perfect image of God. And this brings us to the critical starting point of our existence. Human beings are made *"in the image of God"* (Genesis 1:26-27). That's where our story begins. The entire temptation leading to the first sin, was an attempt to <u>be</u> like God; that's what the tempter said, *"For God knows that when you eat of it your eyes will be opened and you will be like God, knowing good and evil."* (Genesis 3:5). When man sinned, he lost the moral likeness, his sinlessness, but he retained the natural likeness of intellect and emotions. So man is, in essence, an image of God.

We should not make any idols or any image of God, instead, God wants us to realize that WE are the image of God!

My life and the life of every Christian is an existence of fellowship with the Spirit of God. To love, adore, trust, believe, and exist only to be a blessing to He who has so greatly blessed us.

Reflection:

1. What do you see as the biggest violation of the Second Commandment?

2. Why do you think some people would turn to objects or statues instead of God?

3. Do you think "religious" jewelry gets a bad rap because of the misunderstanding of graven images?

4. Knowing that God is watching us lovingly, day in and day out, are there any 'idols' you feel you need to get rid of in your life?

Willis A. Bullard

THE THIRD COMMANDMENT

Recommended Scripture Reading: Exodus 2:23 – 3:15; Matthew 5; Matthew 15; James 1

THOU SHALT NOT TAKE THE NAME OF THE LORD THY GOD IN VAIN (KJV).

Oh how this commandment is destroyed daily by believers and non-believers alike. "*You shall not misuse the name of the Lord your God, for the Lord will not hold anyone guiltless who misuses his name.*" Deuteronomy 5:11

Many Hebrew scholars tell us that the word translated "name" refers to the character or reputation of the one who bears it. So if I were to re-write this commandment it would start with "You shall not misuse the character or reputation of the Lord your God.

The revealed or spoken name of the LORD, can be understood as a prayer calling for the very presence of God Himself. The word translated "in vain" probably comes from another word that pictures a rushing and destructive storm (sho-ah). One way to understand this mitzvah, then, is that we should never invoke God's name in a thoughtless, careless, or "stormy" manner whether with our own words or – hang on tight – with our actions.

In other words, when we call upon the Lord, we are actually invoking the one true God of the universe to manifest Himself to us. Since God is faithful and will be true to His name, He is present whenever He is called. This is serious business, and we should never take it lightly. Let me slow this down. When we call out to God – HE WILL BE THERE. He will remain true to the calling out of His name. This is a powerful tool available to all who believe.

But as this society slowly pulls away from the acknowledgement of the True God and as churches become more "society-sensitive" and "politically correct", we have become a society that takes God's name in vain by hypocrisy or making a profession of God's name, but not living up to that profession. Those that call upon the name of God but do not depart from sin or evil, as that name binds them to do, call out in vain. We profess the name of God with our lips, but deny him with our words, our lifestyle, or even our actions and thus we make our worship vain.

"You hypocrites! Isaiah was right when he prophesied about you: 'These people honor me with their lips, but their hearts are far from me. They worship me in vain; their teachings are merely human rules…" Matthew 15:7-9.

Even our religion is vain, *Those who consider themselves religious and yet do not keep a tight rein on their tongues deceive themselves, and their religion is worthless.* James 1:26.

We take God's name in vain by not keeping our word. If we make a bond with God, a promise as men and women of God, we bind our souls with those promises. When we break those promises, we have taken his name in vain. You know those promises: the oath of marriage, the commitment of following Christ, that calling out that you will follow God forever if he helps you with your test. *Again, you have heard that it was said to the people long ago, 'Do not break your oath, but fulfill to the Lord the vows you have made.'* Matthew 5:33.

But it is not just our calling out to God or the words we speak that causes us to violate this commandment. It is our actions, or more correctly our inaction. We take God's name in vain by not following up on our promises. We take God's name in vain by misrepresenting him in the grocery store line when we have over fifteen items in the express lane. Yes, it is that easy to violate God's command especially when we have not been taught the definition of these Commandments. All these years I thought this Commandment was to keep me from saying bad words. Eye opening isn't it?

Everywhere we go, we carry the name of God with us. That is because when we are baptized we are given the commission: *"Therefore go and make disciples of all nations, baptizing them in the name of the Father and of the Son and of the Holy Spirit..."* (Matthew 28:19).

We misuse the name of God when we live and speak and act in ways unworthy of our calling. When we are dishonesty, angry, bitter, sexually immoral, drunk, and more – and that, sadly, just described a Friday night in America. The name of God is misused when we live and speak and act in ways that cover the name of God with shame or dishonor. When our way of life empties the name of God of its glory, that blasphemy is ours.

Can we do this though? Can we live without bringing dishonor to God's name? Yes, and even though it is hard enough to keep our tongue from uttering words against God, with genuine love it is possible to live for God by keeping our words and actions holy. It just takes practice.

Reflection:

1. Our words and our actions can bring shame and dishonor to God. Is this Commandment impossible to live with?

2. Many of us may have used some poor language in the heat of the moment. But today's norm is stringing together profanities. How does poor language affect your witness?

3. We are in a movie theater and the movie that is playing unexpectedly is filled with foul language, sex, and violence. What does that say about us if we do not get up and walk out?

Willis A. Bullard

THE FOURTH COMMANDMENT

Recommended Scripture Reading: Exodus 5: 1-9; Leviticus 25; Acts 1 & 8; 2 Timothy 3.

<u>REMEMBER THE SABBATH DAY, TO KEEP IT HOLY (KJV).</u>

The greatest of all church separators. "*Observe the Sabbath day by keeping it holy, as the Lord your God has commanded you. Six days you shall labor and do all your work, but the seventh day is a Sabbath to the Lord your God. On it you shall not do any work, neither you, nor your son or daughter, nor your male or female servant, nor your ox, your donkey or any of your animals, nor any foreigner residing in your towns, so that your male and female servants may rest, as you do. Remember that you were slaves in Egypt and that the Lord your God brought you out of there with a mighty hand and an outstretched arm. Therefore the Lord your God has commanded you to observe the Sabbath day*". Deuteronomy 5:12-15.

The word translated "remember" or "observe"

means more than merely recalling something past, but suggests the act of focusing the mind upon something in the present. But what are we to "remember?"

Genesis 2:3 *"And God blessed the seventh day and made it holy because on it he rested from all the work of creating that he had done."* We are told that God rested from His creative activity and set apart the seventh day as a memorial of the work of His hands. God called the seventh day "holy" (kadosh), which means set apart as sacred; set apart as exalted and honored.

Just as the Lord set apart a time to focus on and honor the marvelous works of His hands, so we are commanded to regularly set apart a time to focus on and honor our own creative life in God. Notice that both God and man are to set apart the Sabbath and share in the glory of this shared creative life. Did you catch that? God observed the Sabbath.

There was a time in America when the modern church and society used to honor the Fourth Commandment. The church lawn was mowed on Saturday afternoon so it would looks its best on Sunday. Potatoes were peeled Saturday night in preparation for Sunday dinner or to share meals at a church potluck. Sunday itself was framed by Bible study and worship services in the morning and an evening service or time of fellowship to close out the day. In between services, families stayed at home and some communities even observed the Sabbath by having stores closed for the day. But of course this occurred mainly in the south (God's favorite part of

America). Something great Christian organizations like Chick-fil-A and Hobby Lobby continue to observe despite protests by people with nothing better to do but complain about Christians.

Sunday was a special day, that special day of the week. The "day of rest and gladness," the "day of the week that became the symbol of religiosity and of eternal rest." Sunday was a day set apart, and we set it apart religiously.

But today it is rare that we set aside any time at all for God. Our lives are so busy we may be able to set aside one day a week if our schedule allows. I would teach the youth that one who is BUSY is Bound Under Satan's Yoke.

But even when we set aside time for God, it is usually not a whole day. God would be lucky to get an uninterrupted morning or just a couple of hours from most of us. We run around frantically getting ready, finding our Bibles, and then pile into the car (or several cars). We walk into the church building with a minute or maybe even two to spare. Then we compose ourselves and quiet ourselves, and then we express ourselves for an hour. Afterwards we visit over coffee and snacks. Then off we go in multiple directions, the rest of the day much like any other day.

How did we get here? It is clear we did not get here through the study of scripture. We surely did not take a close look at our traditions and matched them up with the Fourth Commandment and ask the critical questions: what should we do; what shouldn't we do; why do we do this; why don't we do this... there is no way the modern church took their doctrine, matched it up against Scripture and said "hey, we have found the right way to observe the Sabbath."

No, what has happened is we got lazy and we dropped the scriptural way largely because we didn't feel like following them anymore, and because we had better things to do with our time, with our Sundays. God's Commandments had become inconvenient.

God has given us an example of Sabbath; after six days of work he rested on the seventh day, took a break, and rejoiced at the work of his hand. We must learn to take a break, and to give him the glory of His works in our lives. *For You, O Lord, have made me glad by what You have done, I will sing for joy at the works of Your hands.* Psalms 92:4.

The Sabbath began when God finished the work of creation. We look to eternity as the everlasting Sabbath in the finishing of the work of providence and redemption as we walk this Earth. And because we live in expectation of the end times, we observe the weekly Sabbath, in honor and remembrance of the Creation and in celebration of eternity. This is our purest act of worship.

God has himself blessed the Sabbath day and sanctified it. He has put an honor upon it by setting it apart for himself and he has encouraged us to expect honor from him in the observance of that day. It is the day which the Lord hath made.

But instead, we have taken the Sabbath and made it disappear. Whether our seventh day is Sunday or Tuesday, we have not held Holy one day in appreciation of the works of His hands. The Puritans are the ones that placed Sunday as the "globally acceptable" day of Sabbath. But it is not the day of the week that matters, it is 'A' day set aside for honoring God that matters. A day where the believer gets that special time to foster a closer relationship with the Creator. It is kind of like date night for married people. You chose a night, any night, and spend it together. Turn off the cell phones. Unplug the television. Just time to spend much needed "get to know each other" time. So it is with God. It doesn't matter what day of the week. But give Him a day!

But even Sunday's have lost their specialness. We have profaned the day God has blessed, honored, and sanctified. We have dishonored it and now society mocks, berates, and even bullies those that hold the Sabbath as holy. What used to be the accepted Sabbath day, Sunday, is not used exclusively for church attendance or reflection of thanks and praise. It is now a regular day used for any of a myriad of entertainment efforts. From professional sports to family picnics to mini-vacations.

And one final thought on this special day. The Sabbath is not the only day to praise and worship God. No, our lives should be open to praise and worship twenty-four hours a day, every day of the year. But what if we are so far off on the meaning of this Commandment and have missed the mark all these years. Read carefully the Fourth Commandment where God has clearly told us to use this day to rest and remember where we came from, not to use it as a family reunion or fund-raiser. If we are not in the house of the Lord on our Sabbath day then spend time, wherever you are giving the Creator glory, honor and praise. Some may go as far as saying our church attendance is violation of this Commandment. Is this Commandment so misunderstood that in fact we must take one day as a stay-at-home thanking God day and then have another day in which we attend church?

My challenge to you is this: find your Sabbath. Find your time to honor God with a day of reflection, praise and adoration. BUT MAKE IT A FULL DAY. Do not work, just reflect on where God has brought you in your walk on earth.

Reflection:

1. It is imperative that we live in the constant presence of the Spirit and we also need the regular practice of worshiping together. Is there one certain day for the Sabbath or is that a personal choice?

2. Have you ever committed one full day to praise and worship? Will you?

Willis A. Bullard

THE FIFTH COMMANDMENT

Recommended Scripture Reading: Leviticus 19; John 19; Ephesians 6; Colossians 3.

HONOR THY FATHER AND THY MOTHER.

The Fifth Commandment marks a transition from the Commandments dealing with our relationship with the Lord to Commandments on our relationship with others. *Honor thy father and thy mother, as the Lord thy God hath commanded thee; that thy days may be prolonged, and that it may go well with thee, in the land which the Lord thy God giveth thee.* Deuteronomy 5:16

The Lord intended that the family would be a picture of His relationship with us. A proper order in the family is the basis for a solid social structure. Just as God created both man and woman in His image, so children are to regard their parents as divinely ordained and truly significant.

The sad reality is today there is very little honor given to parents. Partly because parents are absent and of course partly because we have a society that promotes promiscuity and rewards or celebrates single-parenthood. Because the family foundation is broken, the solid social structure does not exist and so chaos reigns. Now the sad news is this is a dilemma that will not soon end. Matter of fact, if we want to be honest about society and the deterioration of the family unit, we can start with the reality of the single parent family soon becoming the norm.

But how is the Christian to address this issue? When a child dishonors their parents by sneaking out of the house and engaging in risky behavior do we shun this child? Do we shun the family? I have personally witnessed churches turning away single parents; chasing out families who have had a teen make a mistake and become pregnant; and turning away families seeking help in raising their children.

Shocked?! This is not a problem just with the unsaved society. It is a problem within the Christian community. I know of youth pastors that were told by their senior pastor of the church to "do whatever you can to have family X leave the church. They are a handful and a distraction."

This is ungodly and not conducive to building strong Christian families. What we need to do is raise up our parents to become better leaders of their homes. Show the family the Biblical role of parents and children. Let them know there is reward for those who focus on the Word of God to raise their families. Show them that a family living in an atmosphere of respect and adoration of the Spirit of God will prosper. The church should help families in their duties as parents and as children, not chase them off so as not to offend other members. Or as one pastor told me, "that family is like a cancer and I don't want it to spread." Oh my, what have we become?

But can we get to the real meat of this Commandment? Many of us are used to hearing sermons on the fifth Commandment as addressed to young children, calling them to obedience. Matter of fact, the New Testament does go in this direction; instructing children to obey their parents. But here is the big surprise; at Sinai, the Commandment is addressed to grown-ups. And it's clear from the rest of the Old Testament that the Commandment is specifically about how grown children are to treat their aging parents. Those that support their parents will find that God, our Heavenly Father, will support them.

So how are we doing with this one America? Have we traditionally taught the lesson so that the children's minister had projects to do with his or her students for mother's day and father's day? Or have we really missed the mark here?

How does society support or take care of the elderly? It is a pretty pathetic sight. Thousands of elderly in poverty. Many thrown into nursing homes and forgotten. Countless being found dead in their homes days after they had passed because no one ever checks on them. Living in ghastly conditions;

eating garbage; how are we doing Christians?

The family that lives by Biblical principles, will survive this temporary existence on Earth as we have learned in scripture. *"Children, obey your parents in the Lord, for this is right. Honor your father and mother (which is the first commandment with a promise), so that it may be well with you, and that you may live long on the earth. Fathers, do not provoke your children to anger, but bring them up in the discipline and instruction of the Lord."* Ephesians 6:1-4.

Those who, in conscience towards God, keep this and the rest of God's commandments, may be sure that it shall be well with them, and that they shall live as long on earth as God sees good for them, and that what they may seem to be cut short of on earth shall be abundantly made up in eternal life.

Can I break off and get personal? There may come a time in your life when you can no longer care for your aging parent. Take time and find a care facility that will be a great surrogate for you. I had to make that tough decision. God, being ever faithful, lead me to a Christian Care Center where their treatment of the elderly clearly is in keeping with the Spirit of the Fifth Commandment. I live without guilt knowing that when I go to see my mother on the weekends, she will be in great physical shape as well as spiritual shape.

Reflection:

1. Why do you think God placed the Commandment to honor parents right after the Commandments on honoring Him?

2. How are we, as a society, handling this Commandment? Are we really caring for our elderly?

3. What can you do this week to honor your parents?

Willis A. Bullard

THE SIXTH COMMANDMENT

Recommended Scripture Reading: Genesis 4; Matthew 5; Luke 1:26-38.

THOU SHALT NOT KILL.

Buckle in because in my research, this is the one I had to stop and pray about the most. *You shall not murder.* Exodus 20:13

According to the Masoretic text, the Hebrew translations notes that the word for kill - "ratsakh" - applies only to illegal killing (premeditated murder or manslaughter) and is never used in the administration of justice or for killing in war. So the King James Version translation as "thou shalt not *kill*" is too broad.

Since man is made in the image of God, his life is infinitely precious and only God Himself has the right to give and take life. But if you look at it in a philosophical manner, why did God only create one man, Adam? After great thought I saw a great teaching point: "God created one man to teach that whoever takes a single life destroys a whole world."[vii]

WOW! Does this not increase the value of a human life? I was so blown away by this revelation that I physically became emotional. Just writing these words brings back those emotions. But the bottom line is that life is precious and the loss of life is tragic and greater in magnitude than I have ever imagined.

But let's look at where we are as a society: as sad as this statistic sounds it is a great snapshot of crime in America – in 2010 there were 5.5 murders for every 100,000 Americans. This is a drastic drop from 1991 where the rate was almost at 10. But this is how the evil one wants us to see the problem with murder. He is so slick that the media and so-called experts bring out numbers that make us all stop and say, "hey, things aren't so bad."

But can I bring a dose of reality to this topic? You know what reality is don't you? It is truth the main stream media doesn't want you to know. But thankfully I am a news junkie and constantly seek the truth, the whole truth, and nothing but the truth.

The murder rates that the government uses to show what a great job they are doing is a façade. Murder or I should say attempted murder is at an all time high and it is getting worse. What is keeping the numbers low is the unknown or unacknowledged factor known as modern technology or modern medicine. Dr. Stephen Thomas of Harvard Medical School and two colleagues from the University of Massachusetts at Amherst and another colleague from the Emergency Medical Services in Lawrence Massachusetts conducted a study that shows improvements in the quality and quantity of medical care over the last forty-years have resulted in an increasing percentage of lives being saved when people are shot or stabbed in an attempted murder. With improvements in emergency vehicle response time, trauma systems, medical technology, and pharmaceuticals, the numbers are deceptively low.

Dr. Thomas and his team looked at the period from 1960 to 1999 and examined improvements in medicine in light of the murder rate and attempted murders. They found that improvements in medicine were responsible for saving an increasing percentage of people who were shot or stabbed. They noted that medical professionals with long experience in emergency room care would not find this conclusion surprising at all, but just common sense.

The number of murders in 1993 was about 23,000. This results of calculations of the murder rate came out to a conservative 8.5 out of 100,000 population. Dr. Thomas estimates that in that same year, that if they were still using 1960s medical technology and response times, the number of murders would have been around 67,000, or a murder rate of 24.8. This shocking figure gives us a much clearer picture of what is happening in America, because the 24.8 rate is a better reflection of the number of attempted murders that would otherwise have resulted in death[viii].

We have a sinful society that does not value life. Instead, America is a country that believes in the "me first" attitude and for the most part people do not look out for each other, but instead care solely for themselves. This selfishness is reflected in the lack of care about another person's life.

Sadly, it takes horrible incidents like the Fort Hood shootings, and the multiple school massacres for us to realize how sick our society has become.

But this Commandment is deeper than what we read. *Ratsakh*, or murder, can be figurative as well as literal. The *Talmud* notes that shaming another publicly is like murder, since the shame causes the blood to leave the face. Even gossip or slander are considered murderous to the dignity of man. The *Pirkei Avot (Ethics of the Fathers)*[ix] states, "The evil tongue slays three persons: the utterer of the evil, the listener, and the one spoken about..." The Lord Jesus also linked the ideas of our words and attitudes with murder in Matthew 15:18-19 – *"But the things that proceed out of the mouth come from the heart, and those defile the man. For out of the heart come evil thoughts, murders, adulteries, fornications, thefts, false witness, slanders."*

A most troubling part of this misrepresentation of this Commandment is our Christian churches sometimes forget to preach how Jesus spoke of this commandment. In Matthew chapter 5 verses 21 and 22 Jesus said: *"You have heard that it was said to the people long ago, 'You shall not murder, and anyone who murders will be subject to judgment.' But I tell you that anyone who is angry with a brother or sister will be subject to judgment. Again, anyone who says to a brother or sister, 'Raca,' is answerable to the court. And anyone who says, 'You fool!' will be in danger of the fire of hell."*

Other major religions also hold to the belief that murder is tied to anger as well as offending others or the act of arrogance towards others. So why do we have such an angry society? Simple, because, just like other examples, we have forgotten the truth behind our laws lie in the Ten Commandments.

Another example of actions contrary to this Commandment is suicide. Every year some 30,000 people in America take their own lives, and suicide is the third leading cause of death for people between 10 and 24 years of age and an epidemic that is growing. There are many examples of people who commit suicide in the Bible and it's clearly a violation of the Sixth Commandment. If murder is the unlawful or illegitimate ending of someone's life, it certainly applies to self-murder.

The most explosive and controversial example of how the Sixth Commandment is violated in our culture today is abortion. Abortion is ending a human life while it's still in the womb. We tend to think that abortion is a modern day occurrence, but the practice of abortion goes back into the ancient world and was addressed by one of the medical world's most influencing figures Hippocrates. Hippocrates lived approximately five-hundred years before the birth of Christ and is best known for being the author of the

Hippocratic oath, the oath sworn by modern day physicians. Within the oath we find these sobering words: " I will neither give a deadly drug to anybody if asked for it, nor will I make a suggestion to this effect. Similarly I will not give to a woman an abortive remedy. In purity and holiness I will guard my life and my art.".

Sadly, by the time Jesus was born, abortion was a common practice throughout the Roman empire. Thankfully, Mary did not believe in abortion.

Even in America's history abortion was legal in the 1840s, with almost one-half of all pregnancies ending in abortion. Unfortunately the Christians were silent on the issue in the 1840s, but the American Medical Association spearheaded legislation to outlaw abortion. Finally, through the influence of the AMA, in 1873 the Comstock Act made abortion as a form of birth control illegal. But of course all that has been changed with the legalization of abortion on demand in 1973 with the Supreme Court's Roe vs. Wade. The shocking news is since that decision there have been over 35-million abortions performed in America. Abortion on demand as it's practiced in our nation today is a clear violation of the sixth commandment.

Why is murder so bad? The book of Genesis shows us: "*So God created man in his own image, in the image of God he created him; male and female he created them.*" Genesis 9:6

"*Whoever sheds the blood of man, by man shall his blood be shed; for in the image of God has God made man*" Genesis

1:27.

Can we live in this society and not break this Commandment now that we see it is tied to our anger? Of course we can. The key to living under the law is to slow our lives down and think before we act. Weigh the consequences of our actions and above all, have a greater respect for the sanctity of life, after all, it is God's own creation.

Reflection:

1. Knowing what we know now about God's law on murder, can we ever justify abortion?

2. Being angry and using harmful words against someone is likened to murder. How does that change the way you feel towards others?

3. It is clear that God's Laws are not impossible, but by following them we do draw closer to Him. Your thoughts?

While Christians Sleep…

THE SEVENTH COMMANDMENT

Recommended Scripture Reading: Genesis 39; Deuteronomy 22; 1 Corinthians 7.

7. THOU SHALT NOT COMMIT ADULTERY.

This Commandment is not about sex in general. It is not about how to do it, or when, or where. It's not about pregnancy or birth control. And it's not about "safe-sex." The Seventh Commandment, *"You shall not commit adultery"* Exodus 20:14, is about one kind of sex, adultery which is not only contrary to the Law of God but applies to both husband and wife. Adultery: that's when two people who are not married to each other are having sex, even though one of them — or both of them — is married to someone else.

The Seventh Commandment has no room for adultery. Adultery, we learn in Leviticus 20, was punishable by death. Actually most people are against adultery. The exception would be the people who are busy doing it. The penalty for adultery was severe: *"If a man is found sleeping with another man's wife, both the man who slept with her and the woman must die. You must purge the evil from Israel. If a man happens to meet in a town a virgin pledged to be married and he sleeps with her, you shall take both of them to the gate of that town and stone them to death—the young woman because she was in a town and did not scream for help, and the man because he violated another man's wife. You must purge the evil from among you."* Deuteronomy 22:22-24

I used this verse because all too often we associate this commandment with marital unfaithfulness and I also wanted you to see how over the years the punishment for this iniquity has lessened if not disappeared. This Commandment is not only a warning to those that are married, but it is also a warning against pre-marital sex. In every person's life, there is a divine plan to provide you with a lifelong partner or a plan in which you are to remain single. It is a matter of listening for God's voice in reference to this aspect of your life. You just have to wait for that person and time.

So now you know if you have sex with someone, even though you are both single, you have committed adultery because that is not your wife or your husband. Harsh? Yes. Impossible? No. Think of this, if our society lived by this simple rule of no sex with anyone but your spouse, where would venereal disease be? Where would unwanted pregnancies be? The Lord Jesus identified the root condition of adultery as a problem of the heart: *"but I say to you that everyone who looks at a woman with lust for her has already committed adultery with her in his heart.* Matthew 5:27-28.

Adultery is an in-your-face show of disrespect since it not only violates the sworn promise of parties to a sacred covenant (marriage), but perverts our union with God Himself. As Paul wrote to the church at Ephesus, "*We are members of his body, of his flesh, and of his bones. For this cause shall a man leave his father and mother, and shall be joined unto his wife, and they two shall be one flesh. This is a great mystery: but I speak concerning Christ and the church…*" Ephesians 5:30-32.

But as hurtful and destructive as adultery is, our society embraces and even celebrates the sin. From our leaders and their confessed indiscretions, to our television and movie screen. No need to go into specifics because we know the sin is real and sadly, it is not going to go away until Christians stand for the moral right and stop supporting the garbage by watching on the television, at the movies, over the radio, etc.

But really, has the silence of Christians really made this Commandment disappear? Thankfully the answer is no because the Commandment remains but societies disregard of the Commandment is something that is blatantly disgusting. Take for example two of the top-rated shows on television: The Bachelor and The Bachelorette… Case closed.

God is a maker and keeper of promises. To be in the image of God is also to be a maker and keeper of promises. But to commit adultery is to break the promises of marriage. It is to violate the image of

God and its promise-keeping character.

We can live in this society observing this law. We must be on guard because the evil one is crafty. It is not only about how we are tempted, but it is also about how we tempt others. What we talk about with others, our joking, reducing people to objects of desire. This is not keeping a healthy, Godly environment.

But understand that the Bible gives us great guidelines to help us keep on guard and it points out the reality of how evil attacks us. *But since sexual immorality is occurring, each man should have sexual relations with his own wife, and each woman with her own husband. The husband should fulfill his marital duty to his wife, and likewise the wife to her husband. The wife does not have authority over her own body but yields it to her husband. In the same way, the husband does not have authority over his own body but yields it to his wife. Do not deprive each other except perhaps by mutual consent and for a time, so that you may devote yourselves to prayer. Then come together again so that Satan will not tempt you because of your lack of self-control.* 1 Corinthians 7:2-5

Proverbs 5 encourages us to "drink deeply from each other; be intoxicated with each other." The Bible is in favor of sex and it shows us marriage is the place for sex; as long as it is your own marriage.

Reflection:

1. Many have said we need to hold Hollywood to tighter standards because they glorify crime, murder, and adultery. What are your thoughts?

2. What are your thoughts on schools giving teenagers birth control aides? Does it violate our belief in the Seventh Commandment?

While Christians Sleep…

THE EIGHTH COMMANDMENT

Recommended Scripture Reading: Genesis 37; Exodus 20:15; Matthew 19:18; Ephesians 4.

THOU SHALT NOT STEAL

Stealing, in the sense of the Hebrew word **ganav**, refers to both the act of carrying off by stealth that which is not one's own (i.e., theft), but also to the deceptive inner disposition that accompanies the action. And, ultimately, that deceptive inner disposition is a form of self-deception. But unless we understand the Hebrew words, we just read this Commandment as *"Thou shalt not steal."* Exodus 20:15

Not many Christians have associated stealing with self-deception or, if I take it a step further, fear. The person that steals is acknowledging that they have a fear that God may not provide their needs and ultimately they deceive themselves into believing they have to go out and gain whatever the item is because they have to do it "on their own." Of course many of those that steal may not even understand that God provides all we need. But the point here is the lack of trust that God will provide coupled with a belief that you have to do it since it is the only way to get it, is contrary to this Commandment.

How many of us also see stealing as not just taking items from others, but how about stealing of time? How many times do we frivolously waste our time during the day (thus stealing it from what we were supposed to do) and then turn around to ask someone for assistance in completing what we failed to complete (thus stealing their time).

How about the person who goes out and spends money on items they do not need? Compulsive buyers. Do they fall into this category of stealing? Absolutely yes! I have seen parents who will spend money on alcohol or cigarettes or lottery tickets and not have money left for groceries for their kids. They are stealing of their own resources leaving the family in a precarious state.

But here is a very deep and somewhat troubling observation. Though, at the time of the presenting of these Commandments, God had allowed the Children of Israel to "spoil" or steal from the Egyptians in a way of just reprisal or divine justice, he did not intend that it should become the precedent allowing them to steal from one another. This command forbids us to rob ourselves of what we have by sinful or frivolous spending, or of the use and comfort of it by sinful sparing or hoarding. We are also forbidden to rob others by invading our neighbor's rights or taking his goods from his person, or house, or field.

Too often theft is seen as a forcible or clandestine act of taking things, but it also includes over-reaching in bargains (I call this taking advantage of the nice store owner by haggling down to a price that gives him no earnings), or not returning what is borrowed or found, withholding just debts, rents, or wages, and an act of absolute disgrace, robbing the public of money that is dedicated to the service of religion or a church.

Our laws do not take kindly to those that steal. Rob a bank or steal the life savings from an elderly victim and notice how limited your courtroom defenses become. I have yet to see someone attempt the temporary insanity defense in a bank robbing crime. And although this seems like a positive things, it really isn't. Our laws are harsh on things because in America we have placed great importance on material things.

This Commandment can be considered cut and dry by applying a worldly definition of theft, but I want to bring you to the same level of "oh-oh I blew it" that I came to when this was revealed to me:

When I am not tithing my money or time, as dictated by scripture, is that stealing?

Yeah, I know! I am preaching to myself and yes, I blew it. But Ephesians 4:28 gave me the stern words that *"Thieves must give up stealing, rather let them labor and work honestly with their own hands, so as to have something to share with the needy."*

Now that doesn't set well with us does it? We are working day in and day out "to have something to share with the needy?" In 1999 I can honestly say that my vocabulary, like the vocabulary of the average person, included phrases like: my house, my car, my guitar, my, mine, yours, his, hers... the list of possessives goes on. But then something strange happened: I got called to the ministry to work with teens. Suddenly my house was now "the hang-out" for teens. My van became the youth van.

The reality was that even though I worked hard to earn money to afford these things, I came to realize nothing would have been possible if it were not for God and thus all things belonged to him. I was just the caregiver. My life changed. Every Thanksgiving I would go to the grocery store and as I was standing in line with my basket of goods, I would signal the cashier that I was going to pay for the person in front of me. Sometimes we would go to the restaurant and I would be moved to pay for someone's meal.

Not taking care of people in need, people who are struggling to get by, not helping (or blessing) as we are able is a violation of the Eighth Commandment. We are not being good stewards of the blessings in our lives and in essence we are stealing from God.

Can we live in this society and obey this Commandment? Well, it is easy to look at "*Thou shalt not steal*" on the surface and live easily abiding by the law, but when you dig a little and see the Commandment calls to take care of our neighbors and share what God has blessed us with; well it is like serving with the Starship Enterprise – exploring strange new worlds, going where no man has gone before… and that is not within our comfort zone. It is going to be tough, but with God, all things are possible.

Reflection:

1. If God has blessed us with everything in our lives, is it stealing when we do not share that gift with others? Like the gift of teaching? Music? Cooking?

2. What gifts has God given to you? Are you sharing that gift?

3. Have you ever thought about doing a random act of kindness? Will you?

Willis A. Bullard

THE NINTH COMMANDMENT

Recommended Scripture Reading: Exodus 23; Luke 3:14; James 4

THOU SHALT NOT BEAR FALSE WITNESS AGAINST THY NEIGHBOR

This is a strong Commandment that, for some time I thought was all about lying. Well actually it is not really about lying per se, it is more about how we should live our lives as God's representatives. Matter of fact, I will go on record to say lying is so evil, it has been one of the greatest causes of ungodliness in the world.

This Commandment, on the surface, is about is a certain type of lying. To use a big word, an equivocating, or any way devising and designing to deceive our neighbor. These are the lies that get people into trouble…BIG trouble. And can I just come out and say this because many of you reading this have experienced this: Christians are notorious for speaking unjustly against others causing harm to the others reputation or worse.

The greatest example of this poison speech is found in the New Testament story of Stephen who was a man filled with the Holy Spirit. By the Holy Spirit, Stephen was a man of deep faith and wisdom. His faith is what helped him withstand the evil that was put upon him. Stephen also lived and spoke a clear testimony to the Gospel. He committed his spirit to God, and even prayed for the forgiveness of his killers.

Stephen was killed by his adversaries because during those days the Gospel was gaining traction. On the day of Pentecost, thousands put faith in Jesus as Messiah. As time went on, the number of disciples grew and grew. Even Pharisees and priests were putting their faith in Jesus. Leading this wave of Holiness was Stephen. He was *"full of grace and power."* He did *"great wonders and signs"* for all to see (Acts 6:8). And the evil one could not stand it so Stephen had to be stopped. So evil was set in motion and a plan was launched that included false accusations against Stephen; false testimony against this innocent man; and finally, as the evil one would plan, a sentence of death.

The evil that guided these men against Stephen is exactly what the Ninth Commandment forbids. The kind of lying that is serious enough to cause death. This kind of lying cost Stephen his life and it took from the kingdom of God a very powerful and popular witness.

Today we see lying at an almost professional level with no repercussions. Lies come in the form of athletes lying about performance enhancing drugs; politicians lying about anything to place them in a favorable light with voters; students lying about why their homework was not completed; drivers lying to police officers about their speed; and the list goes on.

But a lie is a lie and the greatest lie is the one that makes God the liar. "*If we confess our sins, he is faithful and just and will forgive us our sins and purify us from all unrighteousness. If we claim we have not sinned we make HIM out to be a liar and his word has no place in our lives.*" 1 John 1:9-10. If we deny out past sin and present guilt, we are deceiving ourselves and mocking God. We are not walking in the light.

This also ties into the other commandments in that if you commit adultery, you are living a lie. If you murder, you are living a lie. If you worship idols… you get the point. But to get back to the original text of the Ninth Commandment – we are prohibited against attesting or swearing falsely against our neighbor. This means in matters of law or civil proceedings as well as a deeper level and that is our responsibility to be great witnesses of the truth. Can any of us say that our neighbors can trust our every word or action as truthful? Are we God to the least of these?

"*The King will reply, 'Truly I tell you, whatever you did for one of the least of these brothers and sisters of mine, you did for me.*" Matthew 25:40

How about the unholy talk within denominations about other denominations? Even the jokes about how we have to be quiet when St. Peter is taking us on a tour of heaven because the Southern Baptists think they are the only ones there can be a stumbling block to young believers.

I think James makes it clear: "*When we put bits into the mouths of horses to make them obey us, we can turn the whole animal. Or take ships as an example. Although they are so large and are driven by strong winds, they are steered by a very small rudder wherever the pilot wants to go. Likewise, the tongue is a small part of the body, but it makes great boasts. Consider what a great forest is set on fire by a small spark. The tongue also is a fire, a world of evil among the parts of the body. It corrupts the whole body, sets the whole course of one's life on fire, and is itself set on fire by hell.*" James 3:3-6

How do we live in accordance with this Command? Simple, love your neighbor – your fellow human – unconditionally. Never speak ill of a person. Never lie about them and cause them undue pain, suffering, or worse. Better yet, be an Ambassador of the Kingdom of God.

Reflection:

1. Is there such a thing as a good lie? Or a good time to lie?

2. If you are on the highway driving and there are no other cars around, if you speed is that lying?

3. Have you ever sat through a sermon where the Pastor or Priest spoke ill about another denomination? Isn't this a violation of the Ninth Commandment?

Willis A. Bullard

THE TENTH COMMANDMENT

Recommended Scripture Reading: Exodus 20; Deuteronomy 5:21; Micah 2:1-5; Matthew 5:28; Romans 7:7; Romans 13:9

THOU SHALT NOT COVET.

"*You shall not covet your neighbor's house. You shall not covet your neighbor's wife or his manservant or maidservant, his ox or donkey, or anything that belongs to your neighbor.*" Exodus 20:17

I would like to just end the devotional now because quite frankly this is one of the Commandments that gets so much grief because it just rubs people the wrong way. So why include it? After all it is so out of touch with how we live today. We don't use Oxen or Donkeys so who would covet those things. Right? Or how about the servant talk, or in some translations, slaves. Well, we don't talk about that anymore and quite frankly it is offensive. Right?

Look, it even lumps in the "neighbor's WIFE" with his "belongings" and "property." It is basically saying your neighbor owns his wife just like he owns his Ox. So the reality is this Commandment should be deemed irrelevant right?

No. The truth is we will find different reasons to disregard this Commandment because it is the one we have the hardest time keeping. And maybe because all the other Commandments address our actions while this Commandment addresses our thoughts. And it is understood the sin usually originates from a wrong desire.

"When tempted, no one should say, 'God is tempting me.' For God cannot be tempted by evil, nor does he tempt anyone; but each one is tempted when, by his own evil desire, he is dragged away and enticed. Then after desire has conceived, it gives birth to sin; and sin, when it is full-grown, gives birth to death." James 1:13-15

This solicitation to evil is in no way from God but from man's own inner lust. Whether we are talking about ogling the neighbors wife or drooling over his new truck or just wanting to "be like them" this is an inner lust pushing you to desire something that was not ordained unto you.

The trend of people, specifically our young people wanting to be like their favorite pop singer or athlete. Sometimes that is not a bad thing; to have a role model to look up to and aspire to be like them or achieve goals like them. But when we see people altering their looks and lifestyle to mimic these "celebrities" it becomes dangerous and close to idol worship.

But let us all heed this warning: do not be deceived! James goes on to tell us *"Every good and perfect gift is from above, coming down from the Father of the heavenly lights, who does not change like shifting shadows."*

I like how Christian recording artist Steve Green sings it:

> *Every perfect gift comes from above*
> *From the Father of lights*
> *From the Lord of love*
> *This joy that I have that I'm singing of*
> *Is from the Lord*

Genesis chapter two is filled with examples of God's wonderful creation. He placed a garden for man with trees that were "pleasant to the sight and good for food." So right off the bat man was given things that were desirable. But desirable in a right sense. The attitude of the heart should be to enjoy what God has created or presented to you.

The problem with coveting is most of the time we do not desire things we don't have but rather we desire things someone else has. I remember growing up in Florida and always listening to the radio on the weekends with my sister. We both loved music and would sit there with a tape recorder waiting for Casey Kasem to play our favorite song. When it came on, we listened to the music, the words, and quite frankly I was pleased with what I heard. But then in high school I saw a band of my peers playing a concert at the school. Bacchus was their name and I saw, for the first time in a live setting, the music I loved being played or a better word would be created. They were good. And I saw two very cool things I had seen on the television but never in real life. A bass guitar and an electric guitar. I coveted those instruments but not in the way King David coveted Uriah's wife. I just wanted to play like two fine musicians.

Coveting is created by an empty spot in one's life that leads to evil actions. This is a part of your life, or a hole, you believe needs to be filled to make you whole. During that time of my life, I had no empty spot. I was just intrigued with music and today I feel I am a fairly accomplished guitar player (although the bass still eludes me). But when King David was bored, he set his eyes and his mind on Uriah's wife and soon the coveting became the 'hostile takeover.'

But I did not scheme to get Brian's bass or Randy's guitar. I saved money over the years and bought my own. This is the positive side of the Tenth Commandment. This was an appropriate desire just like one would have the desire to have a faithful and loving wife or husband. The desire that moves you into positive action or creative energy rather than a path of crime or debauchery.

We can live in society while obeying this law. We must change our attitude to be one where our desire is to do all things for the good of God. Our desire is not for my neighbor's 'goods' but for my neighbors 'good'. Our relationship with God must be the sole governor of our sometimes out of control minds. It is the Holy Spirit and the presence of the Almighty along with our life with Jesus Christ that will keep us living in a way that blesses and protects rather than disrupts and harms our neighbors.

The commandments, "You shall not commit adultery," "You shall not murder," "You shall not steal," "You shall not covet," and whatever other command there may be, are summed up in this one command: "Love your neighbor as yourself." View the creation from the eyes of the Creator – an innocent work of beauty. Love does no harm to its neighbor. Therefore love is the fulfillment of the law. Romans 13:9-10

Reflection:

1. What is the difference between coveting and a genuine desire?

2. This being the only Commandment that does not deal with a physical or visible action, does it mean we can hide our indiscretion better?

3. Some cultures believe if someone says they like your (name of item here) you are to give them the (item) so that they cannot violate the Commandment. Your thoughts?

While Christians Sleep…

CAN WE LIVE UNDER THE TEN COMMANDMENTS?

The answer is, '**YES**,' we can all live under the auspices of the Laws of God. But it takes love, joy, peace, forbearance, kindness, goodness, faithfulness, gentleness and self-control.

Look, we have to face the reality that evil has entered every aspect of our existence; not just the physical but the intellectual and the emotional. But we can overcome this by first realizing we do not live day-to-day trying to achieve victory... victory has been handed to us on the cross upon which our Savior died.

We have fallen short of the demands of the Ten Commandments – our world is a 24/7 world that does not stop to observe a Sabbath; modern idols are very real albeit less obvious than those during the days of Moses; we worship money, power, fame, and sex; adultery has effected millions of lives and abortion is alive and well – unlike their innocent victims.

But instead of bringing this devotional to an end discussing what a mess our world is in, I want to lift you up. I want God's Word to lift us all up. We need to embrace God's Laws and encourage all believers to stand firm and look to the cross as our hope. Jesus did all the tough work. All we need to do is obey the

Laws of our Father and remember that no one makes it to heaven unless it is through Christ Jesus our Lord and Savior.

Let us find comfort in God's Word daily and take time to appreciate all that God has given us. If you need reminders I implore you to grab friends or family, armed with Bibles, and head out to some of our countries beautiful open spaces, spread out a picnic blanket and sing out Psalms to the Heavens. Sounds corny but imagine a Sabbath outing in the mountains of New Mexico or the coast of Florida, just you, your family, and God's Word.

Am I a hapless romantic? Maybe. But I am a wide awake Christian who will no longer allow evil to trick or tempt me into disobeying any of God's Commands. Will it be easy? No, but if life on earth were easy would there be any need to strive for Heaven?

We are even warned that we will suffer trials and temptations in the Letter of James to *"Consider it pure joy, my brothers, whenever you face trials of many kinds..."* So no, this is not going to be a cake-walk and yes, we will find ourselves stumbling occasionally. But how comforting it is to KNOW who God is in our life and to understand his Laws for each of us.

My question at the beginning was: Can a person live in today's society observing the laws as detailed in the Ten Commandments? Are the Ten Commandments relevant to the Christian life today? I hope we are in agreement and answer with a resounding yes.

Jesus teaches us in Matthew 5:17-20:

"Do not think that I have come to abolish the Law or the Prophets; I have not come to abolish them but to fulfill them. For truly I tell you, until heaven and earth disappear, not the smallest letter, not the least stroke of a pen, will by any means disappear from the Law until everything is accomplished. Therefore anyone who sets aside one of the least of these commands and teaches others accordingly will be called least in the kingdom of heaven, but whoever practices and teaches these commands will be called great in the kingdom of heaven. For I tell you that unless your righteousness surpasses that of the Pharisees and the teachers of the law, you will certainly not enter the kingdom of heaven."

The Law is as relevant today as it was with the Israelites in the wilderness. The Commandments teach us about life in the Kingdom of God as we are guided on the journey He has prepared for us. We have to live with the understanding that the Ten Commandments are not a set of rules showing us how to live in order to receive God's grace. Instead, the Commandments show us how we should live as people who know God's grace as it is revealed in Jesus Christ.

MATTHEW 22:36-39

Teacher, which is the greatest commandment in the law?

Jesus replied, *"Love the Lord your God with all your heart and with all your soul and with all your mind. This is the first and greatest commandment. And the second is like it: 'Love your neighbor as yourself..."*

Willis A. Bullard

ABOUT THE AUTHOR

Willis Bullard is a recovering youth pastor. Having served in the youth ministries since 1985 he is blessed to see many of the teens with which he has ministered either entering the ministry or remaining involved in their local church.

Willis retired from the U.S. Army in 1998, worked in the corporate world for a few years and then answered God's call to full time ministry in 2003 by walking away from a six-digit income to serve God in what he describes as "the best decision I ever made". Although not currently working in a church, Pastor Will (or P-Will as the teens call him) continues to mentor young adults and teens and has been honored to officiate many of their weddings as well as speak at youth events and other public gatherings.

Will is married to the love of his life, Maria and together they have raised two incredible children who are following God's calling in their own lives. If you are interested in having P-Will speak at your youth or church event, contact him through the website: http://willbullard.wix.com/tencommandments

---

[i] Commencement speech to Duke University, 1987, "The Vannatizing of American Society"

[ii] From Wikipedia, the free encyclopedia

[iii] Bhikkhu Bodhi (translator) (2000), *The Connected Discourses of the Buddha: A New Translation of the Samyutta Nikaya*, Boston: Wisdom Publications, ISBN 0-86171-331-1

[iv] Tambi-Piḷḷai Isaac Tambyah (1925). *A Comparative Study of Hinduism, Buddhism, and Christianity*

[v] The Major Sins Al-Kaba'r By Muhammad bin 'Uthman Adh-Dhahabi, rendered into English by Mohammad Moinuddin Siddiqui

[vi] Adonai is the name used in Judaism instead of the unspeakable name of God. A form of ultimate honor and respect the faithful place on God.

[vii] Mishnah, A description of Judaism's primary book of Jewish legal theory.

[viii] Murder and Medicine: The Lethality of Criminal Assault, 1960–1999, *Homicide Studies*, May 2002, Vol. 6, by Anthony Harris, PhD Department of Sociology, U-Mass, Stephen H. Thomas, MD MPH Division of Emergency Medicine, Harvard Medical School, Gene A. Fisher, PhD Department of Sociology, University of Massachusetts Amherst, and David J. Hirsch, BS Emergency Medical Services, Lawrence, Mass.

[ix] Pirkei Avos: Ethics of the Fathers (Artscroll Mesorah Series)

[x] "That's Where the Joy Comes From" from the Album *He Holds the Keys* – by Steve Green, Sparrow Records, 1986